Our Senses
Smell

Kay Woodward

HODDER
Wayland

an imprint of Hodder Children's Books

Our Senses
Hearing ● Sight ● Smell ● Taste ● Touch

For more information on this series and other Hodder Wayland titles,
go to www.hodderwayland.co.uk

Senses – Smell

Copyright © 2005 Hodder Wayland
First published in 2005 by Hodder Wayland,
an imprint of Hodder Children's Books.

Commissioning Editor: Victoria Brooker
Consultant: Carol Ballard
Book Designer: Jane Hawkins

British Library Cataloguing in Publication Data
Woodward, Kay
   Smell. - (Our Senses)
   1.Smell - Juvenile literature
   I.Title
   612.8'6

ISBN 0750246715

Printed in China by WKT Company Ltd

Hodder Children's Books
A division of Hodder Headline Limited
338 Euston Road, London NW1 3BH

Cover: A girl smelling flowers.

Picture Acknowledgements
The publisher would like to thank the following for permission
to reproduce their pictures: Alamy 9 (Christa Knijff/Royalty-
Free); Corbis 4 (Norbert Schaefer), 5 (O'Brien
Productions/Kevin Cozad), 7 (James Leynse), 8 (Saba/Najlah
Feanny), 12 (Sygma/Baumgartner Olivia), 13 (Walter
Hodges), 15 (Massimo Mastrorillo), 17 (Paul A. Souders),
Imprint page and 18 (Philippe Eranian), 19 (Kennan Ward);
Getty Images *Cover* (Taxi/Dana Edmunds), 10 (White
Packert), 14 (Photographer's Choice), 20 (The Image
Bank/Luis Castaneda Inc), 21 (Stone/Rosemary Calvert);
Shout 16 (John Callan); Wayland Picture Library *Title page,*
11, 22 and 23. The artwork on page 6 is by Peter Bull.

Contents

Words in **bold** can be found in the glossary on page 24.

Smells all around!

The world is filled with **smells**. Different things give off different smells. Flowers and fresh bread smell nice. Rotten eggs and rubbish bins smell nasty.

Our **sense** of smell allows us to take in the amazing smells all around. We use our **noses** to smell. We also use our noses to breathe. Air and smells go into the nose through holes called **nostrils**.

How we smell

Smells travel through the air and up your nose. **Information** about these smells then goes to your brain. This is how you smell things.

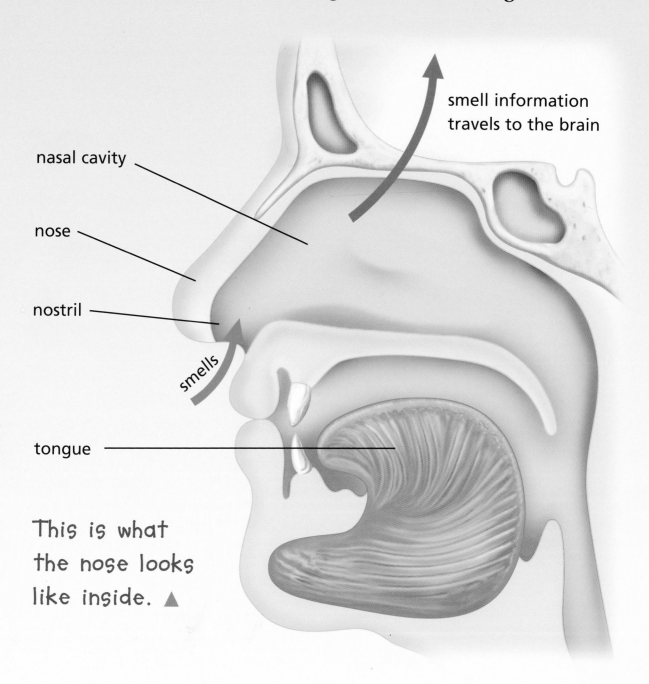

smell information travels to the brain

nasal cavity

nose

nostril

smells

tongue

This is what the nose looks like inside. ▲

Sniffing deeply makes it easier to smell something. The nearer you are to something, the stronger its smell will be.

Nice smells

Food smells so delicious it makes you want to eat. Pizza, popcorn and oranges smell good. Chilli smells spicy. Hot chocolate smells sweet.

Outdoors, there are many amazing smells.
Trees, plants and flowers smell beautiful.
The sea smells salty. Fresh air smells crisp
and clean.

Different smells

Everybody is different. We all have our own sense of smell. This means that we like the smell of some things, but don't like the smell of others.

▼ Not everybody likes the smell of fish!

Some people might love the smell of onions. Other people might love the smell of strawberries. What do you like to smell?

Smelling

As people grow older, they find it harder to recognise smells. If your nose is blocked when you have a cold, you may not be able to smell properly.

Some people cannot smell at all. This can happen because of an accident or illness. People with no sense of smell find it difficult to taste too.

▲ The senses of smell and taste are linked.

Bad smells

Our sense of smell sometimes tells us when food is bad. Mouldy food smells bad. Old milk smells sour. This means that they shouldn't be eaten or drunk.

Cars pump smelly, smoky air out of their exhaust pipes. In busy streets, the smell and smoke grows worse. This is called **pollution**.

▲ There is lots of pollution in Bangkok in Thailand.

Danger!

▲ Gas has a very strong smell.

Some smells warn us of danger. A **gas** leak could lead to a huge **explosion**. If you ever smell gas, you should tell an adult at once and they will check it out.

When there are flames, there is always smoke. If you smell smoke, you should tell an adult or dial 999 to call the fire brigade. You might save a life.

Fire can be very dangerous. ▶

Animals

Dogs have an amazing sense of smell. They can smell much better than humans. Specially **trained** dogs are brilliant at finding and rescuing people in the snow.

Polar bears use their sense of smell
to find food. They can smell seals
from over a kilometre away.

Minibeasts

Most insects pick up smells with their antennae. These are two long, thin body parts that stick out of the insect's head.

Insects send information to each other using different smells. They give off one smell if they are looking for a **mate**. They give off another smell if they are looking for food.

◄ These ladybirds are saying hello!

Can you smell what it is?

Find out how good your sense of smell is with this simple experiment. Ask your friends to join in. Make sure you have an adult to help you.

1. Gather together lots of different smelly things. Here are some ideas:

   Oranges
   Coffee beans or granules
   Onion
   Chocolate
   Soap
   Cheese
   Scented candle